© 2003 by Barbour Publishing, Inc.

ISBN 1-59310-129-5

Cover design by Julie Doll

Published by Humble Creek, P.O. Box 719, Uhrichsville, Ohio 44683

Printed in China.
5 4 3 2 1

Be My Valentine

DEBORAH BOONE

HUMBLECREEK

INSPIRATION FOR LIFE

*Love one another deeply,
from the heart.*

1 PETER 1:22

In our life there is a single color,
as on an artist's palette,
which provides the meaning of life and art.
It is the color of love.

MARC CHAGALL

Bits and pieces of satin ribbon, touches of delicate white lace, a few dabs of glue, and lots of love soon become a carefully crafted heart. . . .

Yet, each February 14, I find myself searching anew for exactly the right words to say:

"Thanks for being such a special friend."

"I care about you."

"I love you."

So with that in mind, as you read through this small token of my friendship, my care, and my love, I hope you'll see that I'm asking you to. . .Be My Valentine.

Love is patient,   love is kind.
It does not envy, it does not boast, it is
not proud. It is not rude, it is not self-seeking,
it is not easily angered, it keeps no record
of wrongs. Love does not delight in evil
but rejoices with the truth. It always
protects, always trusts, always
hopes, always perseveres.
Love never
fails.

1 CORINTHIANS 13:4–8

Love..

What is love?

No one can define it.

It's something so great,

only God could design it.

Yes, love is beyond

what man can define.

For love is immortal.

And God's gift is divine.

Author Unknown

Let love and faithfulness never leave you. . . .

Write them on the tablet of your heart.

Proverbs 3:3

Came but for friendship,
and took away love.

THOMAS MOORE

The best and most beautiful things in this world

cannot be seen or touched,

but must be felt with the heart.

<small>HELEN KELLER</small>

❤   ❤   ❤

I continue to marvel

how my love for you grows stronger every day.

Just being with you makes me glad!

Let us love one another,

for love comes from God.

1 JOHN 4:7

❤   ❤   ❤

To get the full value of a joy,

you must have somebody to divide it with.

MARK TWAIN

♥ ♥ ♥

Every man feels instinctively that all the beautiful sentiments in the world weigh less than a single lovely action.

JAMES RUSSELL LOWELL

♥ ♥ ♥

Many waters
cannot quench love;
Rivers cannot wash it away.

SONG OF SONGS 8:7

There is no remedy for love

but to love more.

HENRY DAVID THOREAU

Whoso loves believes the impossible.

ELIZABETH BARRETT BROWNING

Where there is great love,

There are always wishes.

WILLA CATHER

We are shaped and fashioned by what we love.

JOHANN WOLFGANG VON GOETHE

❤ ❤ ❤

Oh, give thanks to the Lord, for he is good;

His love and his kindness go on forever.

1 CHRONICLES 16:34 TLB

❤ ❤ ❤

I'm so delighted
the Lord brought you into my life!

We cannot really love anybody with whom we never laugh.

AGNES REPPLIER

♥　♥　♥

This is the day the LORD has made;

Let us rejoice and be glad in it.

PSALM 118:24

We have a God
who delights in
impossibilities.

ANDREW MURRAY

Life is to be fortified by many friendships.

To love and to be loved

is the greatest happiness of existence.

SYDNEY SMITH

❤   ❤   ❤

There are many things in life that may catch your eye,

but only a few will catch your heart.

AUTHOR UNKNOWN

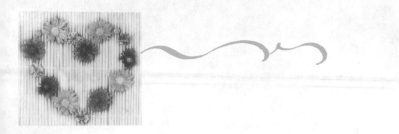

❤ ❤ ❤

*Only love lets us
see normal things
in an extraordinary way.*

ALEJANDRO DE SALMINIHAC

❤ ❤ ❤

18

Roses are red. . . .

The rose speaks of love silently,

in a language known only to the heart.

AUTHOR UNKNOWN

If I had a rose for every time I thought of you,

I'd walk through a garden forever.

AUTHOR UNKNOWN

Flower-filled meadows are God's way of letting

the earth laugh aloud. Let's walk through a meadow

together and join in the laughter!

For, you see,

each day I love you more,

Today more than yesterday,

And less than tomorrow.

ROSEMONDE GERARD

Violets are blue. . . .

If there ever comes a day

when we can't be together,

Keep me in your heart,

I'll stay there forever.

WINNIE THE POOH

The LORD watch between thee and me when

we are absent one from another.

GENESIS 31:49 KJV

Your life and my life
flow into each other as wave
flows into wave, and unless there is peace
and joy and freedom for you, there can be
no real peace or joy or freedom for me.

FREDERICK BUECHNER

Even in those times when the busyness of life pulls

us in different directions, the awareness is

always there that when our tasks

are complete we will again

find the richness of

rest in each

other.

One word frees us of all the weight and pain in life.

That word is love.

SOPHOCLES

Love comforteth like sunshine after rain.

WILLIAM SHAKESPEARE

Love is something   like the clouds that

were in the sky before the sun came out. . . . You cannot

touch the clouds, you know; but you feel the rain and

know how glad the flowers and the thirsty earth are

to have it after a hot day. You cannot touch love

either, but you feel the sweetness that it

pours into everything.

ANNIE SULLIVAN

Sometimes it is in quiet solitude that I sense your

presence most. It is then I am so aware of the joy you

have sprinkled all around me.

To love is to

place our happiness

in the happiness of another.

GOTTFRIED WILHELM VON LEIBNIZ

❤ ❤ ❤

I have spread my dreams under your feet;

Tread softly because you tread on my dreams.

WILLIAM BUTLER YEATS

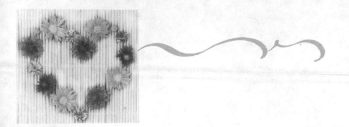

I wrote your name in the sand,

But the waves washed it away.

Then I wrote it in the sky,

But the wind blew it away.

So I wrote it in my heart,

And that's where it will stay.

AUTHOR UNKNOWN

Love does not consist in gazing at each other,

But in looking outward together in the same direction.

ANTOINE DE SAINT-EXUPERY

But the fruit of the Spirit is love, joy, peace, longsuffering,

gentleness, goodness, faith, meekness, temperance. . . .

If we live in the Spirit, let us also walk in the Spirit.

GALATIANS 5:22–23, 25 KJV

Our echoes roll from soul to soul

And grow forever and ever.

ALFRED, LORD TENNYSON

Love is

a canvas furnished

by nature

And embroidered

by imagination.

VOLTAIRE

When you love someone

all your saved up wishes start coming out.

ELIZABETH BOWEN

Let's stand side by side
and gaze out at
the future together.

29

What a grand thing,
to be loved!
What a grander thing still,
to love!

VICTOR HUGO

Where your treasure is,

there your heart will be also.

❤   ❤   ❤

I never knew how to worship until I knew how to love.

HENRY WARD BEECHER

If you live to be a hundred,

I want to live to be a hundred minus one day,

so I never have to live without you.

WINNIE THE POOH

❤ ❤ ❤

Love is happiest when
it's shared,
and I'm so blessed
to share mine with you.
Happy Valentine's Day!